For Sienna

Harry The Starfish

MollyReuben

Harry The Starfish

Rhymes rhymed by Kevin Oakley
Pictures painted by Molly Reuben

First published in Great Britain in 2013
on behalf of the author
by Scotforth Books
www.scotforthbooks.com

Copyright © Kevin Oakley and Molly Reuben 2013

Printed in Great Britain by Short Run Press

ISBN: 978-1-909817-03-6

Sit down on a comfy cushion, listen to my story,
Of dreams, of friends, of jellied eels and sometimes things quite gory.
Dreams can be achieved and they can change your life as well,
Catfish, is my name and this is what I have to tell ...

Harry was a starfish, who loved to sail the seas,
He loved the rolling waves and he loved the salty breeze.
Whether it was stormy or calm as calm could be,
Harry was contented all the time he was at sea.

He sailed a ship to Singapore and jumped a junk to Durban,
He got a lift to Goa from a man who wore a turban.

He learnt "hello" in Old Shanghai, to all he said "Ni hao",
Then, "Ha salik alaikam" when he sailed upon a dhow …
(That's hello in the Maldives where he found himself last year,
He went there for a rest amid the waters, oh, so clear).
While there, he swam in turquoise waters humming to himself,
Until he saw a great big rock cod on a coral shelf.

The cod just sat there staring, he had eyes as big as plates,
"OK chum?" he suddenly said "I'd like us to be mates."
"You see I'm not from round these parts, I washed in on the tide,
And looks to me you're new in too, so let me be your guide."

Harry looked him up and down, the cod seemed very keen,
And Harry being kindly didn't want to be thought mean.
But on his travels he had learnt to always take great care,
And so said "Why I thank you but I don't know if I dare."

"Dare!", exclaimed the rock cod with a huge and toothy grin,
"Do you think I'd eat you? 'Course I wouldn't ... shake my fin.
In any case it happens that about an hour ago,
A dozen tasty squid came by and well ... best you don't know."

So Harry thought he'd take a chance and shook fins with the cod,
Who smiled and said "That's great, now little starfish, call me Todd."

They toured the local reef and looked at all there was to see,
And then ate chewy kelp stalk chips and plankton dips for tea.

Harry met Todd's closest friends . . . ,

there's Una who's a tuna,

. . . Cass the wrasse . . .

Then Ray (a ray) . . .

. . . and Slash (a barracuda).

A rough and ready lot they looked but friendly to the core,
And if you got in trouble well they knew what mates were for!
A sea-Colada drink then set young Harry's head a spinning,
He said "I think I'll turn in now", but Todd just sat there grinning.
Harry gave a gulp and thought "Well, now I'm in a bind."
Nervously he watched as Slash moved quietly round behind.

Ray said "We've been thinking, why a little star like you,
Keeps moving round the oceans like old Todd tells us you do."
"Yeah", said Slash, "Why is it you don't lie low in the kelp?
Is there something that you did? Is there some way we can help?"

"Oh no" said Harry "There's no problem, please don't hurt a soul."
"Sole!" said Slash "A flat fish, so then that will be my goal.
That's OK, I've dealt with huge great flat faced fish before,
They look up with their big sad eyes then … vroom … they're out the door."

"No, no" said Harry "That's not it, I move at my own pace.
I came because I thought it time to move from my last place."
"Plaice!" said Slash "Just don't get started, you think sole
    are mean?

Plaice are really just about the worst fish I have seen."
Harry looked at Cass and whispered "Is Slash such a bounder?",
"No" she said, "It's just his dad ... he ran off with a flounder.
So Slash now thinks that all flat fish are rotten to the core,
Its best if you don't mention flat fish to him anymore."

I should add barracudas aren't all rough, tough and uncouth,
But I heartily advise you not to stray too near a tooth.
Their tempers are much shorter than an angry tiger shark,
And as the saying goes their bite is much worse than their bark.

So Harry thought again and chose his words with utmost care,
"No one makes me move from town to town, to be quite fair.
It's me you see, I cannot stop. I must fulfil my wish,
And that is why I move from ship to ship and fish to fish.
Most starfish like to stay quite still and only move to eat,
But since I looked up to the sky I've had five itchy feet.

I've searched the oceans cold and hot to find the right solution,
Through waters clear as jellyfish and some filled with pollution.
Stars of many kinds I've seen all colours, hues and sizes,
And talked to most but even so I still can't reach my prizes.

For when its dark I look straight up into the night-time sky,
To see a thousand stars all twinkling down as they glide by.
And in my heart I know its true, if I'm to feel quite free,
I'll have to reach up high … a twinkling star is what I'll be."

Well Slash he sniggered, Cass just smiled and Todd he looked aghast,
But Ray said "I've an idea but I'll have to shoot off fast."
With that he whipped his spiky tail and vanished out the door,
Shouting "All meet up at Todd's, I'll see you there at four".

They all split up to have a think and said they'd meet up later,
A hive of fishy thinking, all along the world's equator.

Ray was strong and flapped his wings so hard he nearly flew,
And in his mind he formed a plan for what he had to do.
It seemed to him the stars just sat there in the night time sky,
And so the problem wasn't staying up there once that high.

Harry needed launching which would take them all their might,
But once he reached the other stars he'd stick up there all night.
Then when he'd had enough, perhaps some time 'round half past eight,
By wiggling all his arms, he would then start to gravitate.

"But how to get him up?", Ray thought, "it's too high
    for a tower",
"That's why we need a huge great bit of rubber for
    some power.

The greatest ever catapult I will
    then engineer,
So Harry can fly up into the dark,
    final frontier.
As Harry takes the greatest step a
    starfish has, for sure,
Out to where no starfish has ever
    gone before!

Ray knew where to find a great big
    stretchy bit of rubber,
(Even silly fish know that the best
    comes from whale blubber).

Whales, though huge, must stay in trim, they can't neglect their weight,
That's why they visit whale weigh stations yearly to deflate.

The nearest whale weigh station was run by the crab, McNab,
And he owed Ray a favour which Ray thought he'd take in flab.

McNab used giant battered scales to check the whales for size,
To see how much to trim off if they'd eaten all the pies!

He used his massive claws to carefully trim off from the whales,
All excessive blubber and to neaten up their tails.

I must explain this process, which might seem a little painful,
Did not hurt the whales who simply sat there quite disdainful.
Blubber is a natural product of the whales' digestion,
Which as it builds up causes whales to suffer indigestion.
Removal is quite simple if one knows just where to trim,
And then the whales all find it so much easier to swim.
McNab is happy as he can then sell the blubber too,
For use in anything from trampolines to Irish stew.

So Ray swam up to old McNab and said "Remember me?
I need 50 yards of blubber … and I want it all for free."
"How much, Laddie?" said McNab, "That sounds too much to me.
How about we haggle and then settle on, say … 3?"

Ray was cross, there wasn't time to haggle with the crab,
He said "For shame, don't you forget you owe me big McNab."
"That I do", the crab looked down "I will not ye' deprive,
But truthfully my total stock is only 25.
Its been a slow year for the whales with not much food, it's grim!
There aren't that many whales who came in for their yearly trim."

Rays face dropped he didn't think that it would be enough,
But thanked McNab and swam off slowly with the springy stuff.
Deep in thought, he didn't look out where it was he swam,
And sure enough he swam into a gently dozing clam.
He shook his head, and looked around and there before his eyes,
He saw the answer to his lack of catapult supplies.

    Big and burly Shirley was a giant squid type girly,
    She sat there putting lipstick on, her tentacles
        all swirly.
    Shirley was biggest giant squid the seas had seen,
    20 metres long and always known to be
        quite mean.
    When small she asked her giant mum if she
        could stay petite,
And when told she'd be a giant she sent out an
    angry tweet.
She always wanted to be short and so as a disguise,
Wore lots and lots of make up and bright corsets
    the wrong size.
She really didn't need to as she always looked so sweet,
The kind of squid another squid would really like
    to meet.

And here she sat in front of Ray, make-up on and sighing,
And just behind her hung her spare red corset gently drying.

She had these corsets made to size to stretch along her body,
Very big and very strong and high class, never shoddy.
The tailor was a swordfish who could sew things with his nose,
Highly in demand for perfect stitching in your clothes.

Ray used a trick that all rays have and in the sand he hid,
Where he waited hidden and watched young Shirley squid.
She used a polished shell to make sure that she looked just right,
Then, satisfied, she jetted off and went out for the night.

Ray swam out and grabbed the corset now the coast was clear,
Then hurried back to Todd's place in case Shirley was still near.

Todd and Harry met Ray swimming to Todd's' rocky home,
And couldn't help but laugh so much they make a bubbly foam.
There was Ray (in corset) slowly swimming on ahead,
A lovely stringy blubber wig streaming round his head.

Slash soon arrived with Cass behind, looking fit to cry,
They couldn't find a ladder that would reach up to the sky.
They had a simple plan to find a ladder (big and strong),
And then to hold it while young Harry simply climbed along.

Although they'd looked in many caves across the coral reef,
They couldn't find a big one and their efforts just caused grief.
As when they finally found one they discovered nothing's meaner,
Than a soapy, wet and angry red faced shouting window cleaner.
"Put that ladder back right now, the two of you just stop",
It's not surprising really. He was still up the top!

But Ray was full of energy, simply rippling with delight,
Announcing "Pack your bags and let's get to the Isle of Wight!
My plans a good one, lets get going. Harry don't you worry,
This humble ray will make your day, now pack I'm in a hurry.

We're heading North, the winters there will make your fins go numb-er,
But if we set off quickly we can be there for the summer."

Todd said "Una, you stay here, look after things and then,
Before you know it we'll be back to see you once again."

So off they went with all good haste as fast as they could swim,
A global trek across the ocean on a starfish whim.

      They swam all week, the current helping, setting quite a pace,
      Till Slash, distracted, chased a large and friendly shoal of plaice.
      They tugged his fins until he stopped and muttered, "Oh OK",
      And everyone, exhausted, rested on the back of Ray.

      Harry glowed with pride at what his new friends did for him,
      The thought of twinkling made him go all tingly in each limb.

Right around the wild Cape Horn and Africa's West coast,
They swum non stop fuelled only by a pack of kelp on toast.
They knew they'd reached the coast of Spain when first they
    Heard the cry,
Of "Hola" as a hundred thousand sardines swum right by.
Then in the Bay of Biscay when a huge storm was a threat,
They were offered cover by a lovely French Crevette.

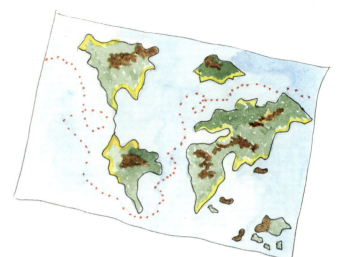

Crevettes are very posh French prawns who run
    their own cafe,
Always pink and pretty and they wear a red beret.
She sung and danced with both claws clapping, fun
    was had all round,
And Todd joined in with fins all slapping, singing much
    too loud.

The storm moved off and Ray said
    "Todd, there's no time for romance,
Once last effort and we'll soon be
    swimming past Penzance.

The English Channel was now close, they set off at first light,
And soon were turning East towards Rays' goal ... the Island of Wight.

They dodged the ships that move all British goods along the Channel,
Tankers full of cheddar cheese, pork pies and yards of flannel.

They also bypassed 3 young men all trying to swim to France,
And only missed a yachtsman shouting "Tally Ho", by chance.

And then they saw the chalky cliffs ahead as clear as day,
They'd reached the Isle of Wight and settled in Freshwater Bay.
Todd caught his breath and looked around and said to Ray "What now?"
And Ray said "Now we wait for star light. Right ... lets find some chow".

"The local grub's quite good here" said a hungry looking Slash,
"I know a place just down the rocks that serves up pie and mash.
Its called 'The Limpets Bottom' and is run by jellied eels,
Their gravy's really nice it goes all dark when it congeals."

They went off to 'The Limpet' and they ordered home made pies,
Full of whelks and winkles, served up with mash or fries.

"And now", said Ray, while wiping drips of gravy from his lips,
"I'll tell you what we're doing here … come on Slash, leave those chips."

They swum along dramatic cliffs and through Freshwater Bay,
And off towards the western tip where Ray turned round to say,
"Have you ever wondered how the Isle of Wight got named?
I'll tell you that it's certainly not the way that men have claimed.

You see, to find the truth you have to get beneath the water,
But men just make up stories they don't do just what they oughta!"
He took them round the headland where some rocks rose pure and white,
"They call these rocks the Needles and they're why we're here tonight.

From up above the water they may look like chalky teeth,
But see, they look much different when you look from underneath."

Sure enough as Harry looked, surprised, he made a sigh,
For rising up in front he saw a massive white rock Y.
"This", said Ray, "is my surprise, the key to Harry's dream.
And from it we're about to make "The catapult supreme!".

Todd let out a laugh and said "Why Ray, you're quite amazing,
Does Harry know he's in for something wild and so hair raising?
And don't forget we've got to keep our Harry safe and sound,
We can't just throw him up and let him squish back on the ground.
And if you think we would you must be right out of your pram!".
"Calm down", said Ray, "It's all in hand, I've sent a Teleclam.
And if the clam got through OK, you'll see in just a mo,
The best solution that there is to falling nice and slow.
A friend from Rhyl said he would help by looking through the bins,
Something not so easy, for us with fishy fins".

Underneath the oceans they don't have the telephone,
The water stops them working be they touch or be they tone.
It used to be, to send a message, letter or a note,
You'd have to find a bottle just to make the message float.
Then cast it out upon the waves and let it ride the sea,
And to your destination it would bob (eventually).

The bottle post was poor the fish all said it was a mess,
Explaining why a mackerel then set up 'Seahorse express'.

For a fee (quite reasonable) your post was whisked along,
By a seahorse ridden by a shrimp in a sarong.

The seahorse post improved things and delays became much fewer,
And an enterprising mullet starting selling the manure.

He collected it by swimming on the route the shrimps were taking,
Looking for manure and collecting it by raking.

But things then got quite nasty after just a couple of years,
A rival mullet started and they boxed each others ears!
The fight alarmed a seahorse and he bucked and ran away,
The prawn could not control him and while shouting in dismay,
He fell right off and as he fell the air it turned much bluer,
He landed on a mullet rake ... a barbequed prawn skewer.

Things had to change, they couldn't have another prawn upset,
So Alexander Graham Clam devised the best scheme yet.
In all the seas were clams just hiding on the muddy bed,
With a jet propulsion unit set into their head.

They never used it, not because they're scared or lazy fish,
They simply had nowhere to go they had all they could wish.
I don't wish to be cruel and so I'll say this very quick,
You see most people think that clams
      are really very thick.

But Alexander wasn't just your average clam, you see,
He wanted to promote the great clam nation through the sea.
He looked clams up and down, examined each and every facet,
Deciding he could put to use their single greatest asset.
He painted up a sign in gleaming red and white emulsion,
"Open Now for Teleclams" sent out by jet propulsion.
Business was soon booming as clams zipped around the world,
Alexander got so rich he had his whole shell pearled.
Teleclams became the standard: 'Postage sent by jet',
Challenged only by the ever growing finternet.

A shadow loomed above the chums, it gave them quite a fright,
But Ray said "Here comes Claude he's right on time, calm down, alright?."

Claude's a crow from Monaco who likes to live in Rhyl,
You see there's lots of chip shops there and Claude can eat his fill.

They all swam over to the shore and there (his beak quite shiny),
Sat Claude, "Bonjour me brave or as zey say round 'ere, Caw Blimey".

Zee story of your bon voyage is spreading though the seas,
To 'elp you is an honour can I shake your fins, yes please?

'Allo friend Ray your message came and gives me time enough,
To look through all zee garbage cans until I finds your stuff.
I 'as it ere besides me and I 'opes that it will suit,
An aerosol of hairspray an some bubble wrap to boot."

Ray said, "Great, and in return to munch on with your chips,
A kilogram of salty winkles, picked up on our trips."

"Ray, my friend, c'est magnifique, but one thing I 'az more,
Zee sticky tape you wanted it is down here on zee shore.
I think I'll stay and watch zee show from on zis pro-mon-tary
And while I munch on winkles I will do a commentary"

"Well now I'm even more confused", huffed Todd to one and all,
"How is tape and hairspray going to help to stop him fall."

Cass whooped "Todd its simple, it's the hairspray that's the key,
Use it like a jetpack and he'll float down gently, see?"
"Yeah", said Harry cheerily, "Let's start right away,
And when I'm back we'll celebrate the genius of Ray."

Well, word was spreading far and wide the crowds were
      growing fast,
And Harry sensed his dream was really coming true at last.

First Harry did some warm-ups so he wouldn't come to harm,
He didn't want his trip in space to strain a leg or arm.
Then Cass and Slash between them dressed him in the safety gear,
A winkle for a helmet and some goggles nice and clear.

Kneepads (4 of those) so Harry wouldn't skin his knees,
A lovely seaweed jumper to keep warm up in the breeze.
Mittens for his hands and (held on by a strap),
A waistcoat to protect his body, made from bubble-wrap..

"Tie the jetpack on as tightly as we can afford",
Said Cass "And then tell Harry just to keep hold of this cord."
(The cord led to the nozzle of the hairspray on his back,
When tugged the nozzle would fall off, starting the jetpack).

Meanwhile, Todd and Ray were busy working off their socks,
Setting the elastic up below the chalky rocks.
They tied a loop in either end and called Claude to their aid,
He flew up to the Needles and he dropped the loops they made.

And so with blubber now secured on both sides of the Y,
They fixed the corset in between as though hung out to dry.
Todd then made a test run pulling fiercely on the corset,
Heading down into the deep sea off the coast of Dorset.

The blubber corset tightened deep down in the Channel flows,
Till Todd, exhausted, let it go and shouted "Thar' she blows."

A massive zingy twangy boinging echoed round the bay,
The corset shot up through the rocks then back the other way.
"Its working fine", said Todd enthralled, "but come the final hour,
We need to pull it further; we will need a lot more power".

"We'll need to get some help then" Ray said "lets see who's around",
And both of them swum up onto a seaweed covered mound.

Word of Harry's journey had now spread both far and wide,
The seabed round the catapult was filled from side to side.
Stalls were selling candied whelks and kegs of ginger beer,
And pictures of our Harry made a perfect souvenir.

Then Todd saw who they wanted (there is almost
    nothing meaner),
A squad of tiger prawns were warming up in an arena.
A sign announced 'The finest fighting prawns of
    Bangalore,
The roughest toughest fighting prawns to fight upon
    the shore.'

Prawns, in case you don't know, make the ultimate sea army,
Their shells are hard, their claws are sharp, when angry they go barmy!
The prawns of Bangalore have long been known as quite the best,
They train all through the winter and they never wear a vest!

Todd went down to find the gleaming Sergeant Major prawn,
With medals shining and a turban perched upon his brawn.
His muscles all had muscles of their own he was so strong,
He shouted "right you 'erberts get a move on, come along."

The tiger prawns began their demonstration. What a show!
Hand to hand in combat, Tae Kwon Do and then Kung Po.

Todd said "Sergeant Major, could I have a quiet word,
I wondered if your squad is quite as tough as I have heard?"
The Sergeant Major peered at Todd, his moustache gave a twitch,
"Just what do you mean", he said and gave his staff a swish.
"The fighting Bangalore is quite the perfect war machine,
They always take their orders and always fight real mean.
'Perfection in a Prawn' is what we have as squadron motto,
We would not leave the squad, not even if we won the lotto.
So when an ugly cod asks if we're tough, he'd better run,
As we're roughest toughest fighting prawns there are, bar none."

"Great", said Todd, "Don't take offence I see you're prime prawn male,
I've come to ask for help to make sure Harry cannot fail."

"Harry?" said the Sergeant Major, "Harry's why we're here.
You should have said before, I want a quick word in your ear.

A plucky little starfish that one, met him once before,
Cruising down a river in the South of Bangalore.

He chased away a spider crab that caught one of my boys,
He hid behind a rock and made a funny squeaking noise.
'Eeeeecky Beeeeecky chuc chuc eeeeecky beeeecky chuc chuc plinner',
Which is shark speak for 'I'd like some crab meat for my dinner'.

The crab he scuttled sideways running scared along the path,
Leaving little Harry and my boys to have a laugh.
Any help you want just let me know and we'll be there,
I'd have offered sooner if I'd only been aware."

So Todd explained about the lack of power from their blubber,
And how they needed muscle to extend the springy rubber.
Sergeant major shouted "Right, we'll soon provide your power",
Then to the fighting prawns he said "Get over here you shower."

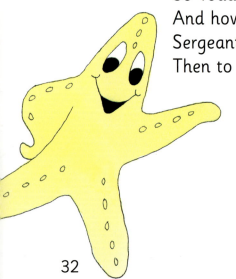

With military precision all the prawns came to attention,
And Sergeant Major told them of the rubbery invention.
They formed a drill line double quick, and marched into position,
Waiting for the Sergeant Major to give them permission,
To pull the catapult with every sinew, at full pace,
And help to launch our little Harry into outer space.

All was set, Ray gave the word and Harry made his way,
Towards the catapult that was about to make his day.
The crowds they cheered and waved and knew that no-one could be braver,
And Claude prepared his commentary, his voice was all a quaver.

The sun then set, the sky was dark the stars were clear to see,
And in between a little space for one more star, Harry.
He reached the corset harness and he jumped in for the ride,
His stomach gave a little jump with butterflies inside.

The prawns with Todd and Ray all grabbed the huge great blubber strip,
Ray said "All get ready" and they took a tighter grip.

The time had come, the countdown started, soon he'd be a hero,
7,6,5 … 4,3,2 then 1 and finally zero.
"Go" said Ray. They ran together taking up the slack,
Down into the sea without a moment to look back.

The blubber corset stretched out more and more and even more!
Harry thought the strain would break the catapult for sure.
The tension grew with every step they all pulled harder still,
The prawns were sweating lots but carried on with iron will.
Todd's tail swished for all he's worth and Ray flapped more than ever,
The blubber started quivering, it's now or else it's never!

A shout from Ray and all got ready,
Harrys' heart it sang,
"Now" said Ray, they all let go and
heard a massive . . .

... TWAANNNGGGG!

Like a rocket Harry raced off trailing streams of bubbles,
Ray and Todd cried "Yes!" It had been worth all of the troubles.
All the crowd they oohed and ahhed or stared in startled state,
And on the cliffs above Claude had begun to commentate.

"Ladies and monsieurs direct your eyes upon the waves,
Harry 'ee is launching to the stars just as 'ee craves."
And sure enough our starfish then flew right out of the ocean,
Past the cliff and upwards as the crowd raised a commotion.
Muscles clapped their shells together, octopi changed colour,
Pipefish piped as shoals of fish all hugged and kissed each other.
"Au revoir my leggy friend" called Claude a little tearful,
"I 'opes to see you once again although I is quite fearful".

Slash and Cass they waved like mad as Harry whizzed straight by,
Todd and Ray met up with them as Cass said with a sigh,
"To think that just a while ago that timid little star,
Was swimming round the oceans, just how did we come this far?"

Of course, our Harry couldn't hear a word that they were saying,
He was getting chilly with his seaweed jumper fraying.
At first when he was fired off he couldn't move an arm,
Accelerating skywards, he was frozen in alarm.

But soon he settled down and started looking round and down,
The Isle of Wight was getting small, lights twinkling in the town.

The crowds that cheered him off were now like ants upon the shore,
And Claude was flying round still Caw-ing till his throat was sore.

Up and up through misty clouds his winkle helmet gleaming,
A shooting star like none before his seaweed jumper streaming.
Up and past the clouds until he reached his sea of stars,
He really was in heaven as he zoomed up close to Mars.
Looking down along the coast he saw white cliffs in Kent,
And all along to Penzance where a holiday he'd spent.

He hung up in the sky a new star on its maiden flight,
And twinkled all his arms upon the darkened Isle of Wight.

Time seemed to stop and Harry felt he weighed nothing at all,
And then his stomach told him he had just begun to fall!

And though he loved his stardom and his spell as star jet-setter,
He knew deep down that with his friends was where he felt much
    better.

So as he fell he felt quite calm and glowed with warmth felt clearly,
The warmth of going back to see the new friends he loved dearly.

Harry looked down as he planned to make a careful landing,
He checked his jet pack once again and tightened all the banding.
Instructions Ray had given at the time had seemed enough,
"When you see us once again just again pull the cord (its tough).
The jetpack slows your fall ensuring when you make your
    splashdown,
It's safe, then we'll be there with breakfast (eggs and beans
    and hash brown)."

Harry felt round for the cord But no! It want there!
He scrambled round behind him but it wasn't anywhere.
The mittens were not helping so he pulled one off his arm,
And felt all round his jumper as his head filled with alarm.
And suddenly he realised just how high he'd really flown,
And down below the rocks looked like a shark toothed landing zone.
He put his hands upon his head the wind rushed passed and roared,
And there upon his winkle hat he found the jetpack chord.
He spun with joy and laughed out loud his fears all quickly sank,
And in his joy he grabbed the chord and gave it quite a yank.

The jetpack gave a piercing scream, hairspray came out full blast,
So Harry shot back up again ... and this time really fast.
Completely out of all control he'd flown right off the handle,
Straight up like a great deluxe marine themed roman candle.
A starfish comet arced across the sky with jet-stream trailing,
Astronomers in Britain, thought their telescopes were failing.
Harrys' smile could not be bigger zooming through the sky,
He'd been a star and now was shooting, letting out a cry ...
"Yee-haw", he shouted spinning round, "this is the best ride ever!
I've never met a ray like Ray he really is so clever."

Happy as a lark he was, a king without a crown,
And then the jetpack spluttered and he started curving down.
A final pop, a cough and sigh, the jetpack had run out,
And Harry fell in darkness not a soul to hear him shout.

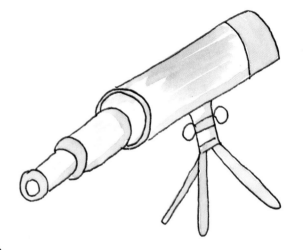

    Over and over he tumbled, down was up then up was down,
    If you had been there too then you'd have seen a starfish frown.
    He tumbled like a catherine-wheel that's come loose from its pole,
    Accelerating earthwards, he completely lost control.

        Faster still he couldn't see a single way of stopping,
        He fell so fast his bubble wrapper jacket started popping.
        The Isle of Wight accelerated back into his view,
        And Harry knew there wasn't anything that he could do.

            His mittens blew right off his, kneepads followed shortly after,
            A starfish in the sky he thought, there's really nothing dafter.

The last thread on his jumper came undone and flew astray,
His popped out bubble waistcoat then flew off and fell away.
The jetpack rattled loose and fell off snapping all it's bands,
Which left his winkle helmet which he clung to with both hands.
This tiny unprotected starfish, winkle hat on top,
Fell down to greet the ocean waves and knew he could not stop.

    And where the air and water meet in constant wavy join,
    Harry hit ... but failed to splash ... instead he just went

... BOINNNGGGGGGG

Up and down he bounced until he really felt quite green,
As though upon a giant fishy ocean trampoline.
And now he heard the crowds all cheering, crying out in glee,
At the safe return of Harry Starfish to the sea.

    As everybody pushed and shoved the sea looked carbonated,
    Bubbles everywhere with creatures totally elated.
    Claude was doing back flips (which for crows is not that easy),
    Cass and Slash kept screaming out until they felt quite queasy.
    The Famous Fighting Prawns let out a round of hip-hooray,
    And even tough old Todd squeezed out a tear or two that day.
    The seaweed bunting tossed and turned amid the churning waves,
    And confetti made from fish scales was released from deep sea caves.

Ray burst through the crowd and said "Well Harry, that's your wish,
And by the way you're sitting on young Kelly Jelly-Fish.
I called her in in-case things didn't go quite as we thought,
And just as well because she's here your troubles came to naught."
"Glad to meet you Harry", Kelly gurgled in delight,
Then drifted off still waving tentacles 'till out of sight.

    So arm in arm the friends strode off, the crowd all gave a cheer,
    And in the Limpets Bottom they drank lots of ginger beer.

So listen well, if you've a wish no matter if it's strange,
Perhaps someone can help you and your wish they can arrange.
With friendship and your own desires you really can succeed,
So reach up for the stars and soon your wishes you'll exceed.
Remember little Harry, tiny star in mighty sea,
Take life by the hand and lead it where you want to be.
My story now is over but I wonder if like me,
You're thinking what the friends are up to out there in the sea.
I'm sure now they're together their adventures will grow greater,
Perhaps they'll send a Teleclam to Mr Catfish, later . . .

The Characters